j507.8
C83c5

Library

Science Fair

DETROIT PUBLIC LIBRARY

LINCOLN BRANCH LIBRARY
1221 E. SEVEN MILE
DETROIT, MI 48203

DATE DUE

FEB 1 5 1997	
MAR 1 2 2001	
APR 1 2	
APR 1 2 2001	

BC-3   3/01

JUL - - 1996 LI

ROURKE
SCIENCE
PROJECTS

SCIENCE IN HISTORY

Authors: George and Shirley Coulter

Rourke Publications, Inc.
Vero Beach, Florida 32964

© 1995 Rourke Publications, Inc.

All rights reserved. No part of this book
may be reproduced or utilized in any form
or by any means, electronic or mechanical
including photocopying, recording or by
any information storage and retrieval
system without permission in writing
from the publisher.

A book by Market Square Communications Incorporated
Pamela J.P. Schroeder, Editor

LIBRARY OF CONGRESS CATALOGING-IN-PUBLICATION DATA

Coulter, George, 1934-
    Science in history / by George & Shirley Coulter.
        p.   cm. — (Rourke science projects)
    ISBN 0-86625-521-4
    1. Science—Experiments—History—Juvenile literature. 2. Science projects—
Juvenile literature. 3. Science—Study and teaching (Elementary)—Activity
programs—Juvenile literature. [1. Science—Experiments. 2. Science projects.
3. Experiments. 4. Science—History.] I. Coulter, Shirley, 1936-   . II. Title.
III. Series.
Q164.C6775 1995
372.3'5—dc20   95-7209
                                                    CIP
                                                    AC

Printed in the USA

JUL - - 1996

The publisher, contractor and author accept no responsibility for any harm that may occur
as a result of using information contained in this book.

TABLE OF CONTENTS

TRAVEL BACK IN TIME AS A SCIENTIST

Do you like to ask questions? Then you already have the makings of a real scientist!

By asking questions, you're taking the first step toward being a scientist. Looking into the past to explore the questions early scientists asked is a good place to start.

Scientists ask questions about why things are the way they are, and then they search and test for the answers. Inside this book, you'll find questions about SCIENCE IN HISTORY. Choose one—or more—that you want to investigate.

After scientists choose a question, they sometimes try to guess the answer, based on their experience. That guess is called a **hypothesis** (hii POTH uh siss). Then they experiment to find out if their hypothesis is right.

Once you choose your question, you'll start to experiment, using the steps written out for you. You'll be acting like a professional scientist, making careful **observations** (ahb zer VAY shunz), and writing down all your results in a **science log** (SII ens LAWG). Your notes are very important. You'll need to use them to make a display to share what you've learned with other people.

Please be careful while you're experimenting. Professional scientists are always aware of safety.

At the end of your experiment, you'll find—answers! Other people will believe your answers because you have scientific proof. However, you don't have to stop there. Your answer might lead to another question. Or you might want to find out about something else. Don't wait. Grab your science log and travel back in time to see some exciting scientific discoveries!

SCIENCE IN HISTORY

Science is all around us. It's not just a separate subject you learn about in school. It's everywhere—in the air you breathe, the games you play, and even in the things your ancestors did.

There could be no science without history. Scientists build on what they already know to make new discoveries. The technology we use today is all based on important discoveries that happened in the past.

Some of the science equipment you use in school was first designed by ancient **alchemists** (AL kem ists). Many of the scientific terms you've learned come from ancient languages that people don't speak anymore.

Up in the night sky, you can see constellations— star pictures—many named by people who lived in ancient Arabia. When rockets streak toward space, they are using scientific principles first used by the Chinese to make fireworks in 1232, and later explained by **Sir Isaac Newton.**

Microscopes, telescopes, cars, radios and television all work on principles first discovered by people who are now a part of history. So the next time you play a video game or turn on your computer, remember— science is a part of you and all you do.

HOW DOES A HOT AIR BALLOON WORK?

Have you ever wondered what it's like to fly? Have you ever flown in a plane before? Way back in the 1400s, **Leonardo da Vinci** made detailed drawings of flying machines. He might even have built some models.

However, it wasn't until 1783 that the **Montgolfier brothers** of France actually lifted off the ground in a hot air balloon—launching humans into flight for the first time!

What To Do

Step 1 Fold a sheet of tissue paper in half the long way. Cut the shape shown in the illustration out of the tissue paper. Unfold the tissue paper and you have your first panel. It should look like a fat tornado. Make three more panels.

Step 2 You'll need a large, flat area to lay out your panels side by side, and probably a friend to help you hold them in place. Run a line of glue along one side edge of a panel about 1/4 inch (.6 cm) from the edge. Stop where the panel starts to slant in.

Glue this first panel to the second by overlapping the edges slightly, and pressing them into place. In the same way, glue the second panel to the third panel, and the third panel to the fourth. All four panels should be laying flat in front of you, with the straight up-and-down edges glued together.

Being careful not to get glue on the other panels, glue the first panel's free edge to the fourth panel.

What You Need

- ✓ 5 sheets of tissue paper— 20 inches (50.8 cm) by 26 inches (66 cm)
- ✓ white glue
- ✓ yard stick or meter stick
- ✓ 24-gauge wire (available at hardware stores)
- ✓ pliers with wire cutter
- ✓ scissors
- ✓ hot air popcorn popper
- ✓ gloves
- ✓ long extension cord— 50 feet (15 m) to 100 feet (30 m)
- ✓ sturdy wood or cardboard box
- ✓ friend to help

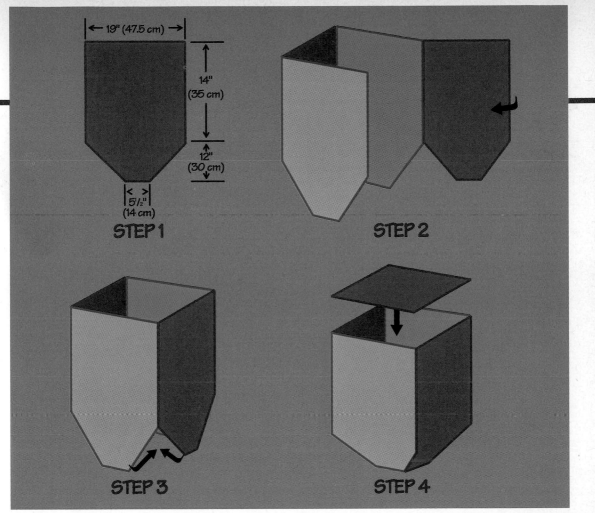

There's more than one way to design a hot air balloon. However, for your first balloon, use this illustration to help you connect your balloon panels together, following the directions in Step 1 through Step 4.

Step 3 Then, glue the bottom parts of the panels together by overlapping the edges 1/4 inch (.6 cm). You'll have to pull the bottom edges toward the middle to make the panel edges overlap. Now you should have an open tissue paper bag, larger at the top than the bottom.

Step 4 Cut a piece of tissue paper 20 inches (50.8 cm) by 20 inches (50.8 cm). This will form the top of your tissue paper bag. Overlap each edge about 1/4 inch (.6 cm) with the top of each panel and glue them together.

Step 5 With your wire cutters, cut a piece of 24-gauge wire 24 inches (61 cm) long. Form a circle by overlapping the ends of the wire 2 inches (5 cm) and twisting them together.

Then hold the wire circle inside the bottom of your tissue paper bag. Fold 1/2 inch (1.3 cm) of the bottom up over the wire and glue it into place.

If the air around you is cool enough, when the balloon is full of hot air it will really tug on your hands. Let go—and it's up, up and away!

Step 6 Take your tissue paper bag and hot air popcorn popper outside on a cold day or cool morning, or inside an air-conditioned gym. (The cooler the air, the better results you'll get.) Place the popcorn popper on a sturdy box, plug it in and turn it on.

Have a friend help you hold your bag over the hot air coming from the popcorn popper. You may want to wear gloves to protect your fingers from the hot air. Keep holding your bag until it fills with air and you feel a real upward tug on your hands. Then, release the bag. Write all your **observations** in your **science log.** You may want to take pictures for your final display. Could you design your own hot air balloon?

Is This What Happened?

Step 6: Your tissue paper bag should have floated up into the air. In a very short time, it should have settled back to the ground.

The molecules of hot air inside your balloon were moving very fast, and got farther and farther apart. Because the hot air inside was less dense than the cooler outside air, the outside air pushed your balloon up, just like water pushes up on an ice cube.

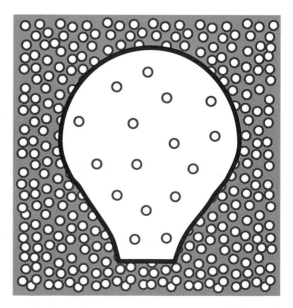

Why?

When you put your tissue paper bag over the popcorn popper, you begin to capture hot air. Air expands when it is heated. That means the **molecules** (MAHL i kyoolz) start to move faster and faster, and farther apart. The **volume** (VAHL yoom), or size, of the gas increases, and so does your balloon.

However, the *amount* of air you have in your balloon stays the same. The air in your balloon weighs the same as it did before you heated it, even though it takes up more space. That means it has a lower **density** (DEN sih tee) than the air outside the balloon. Your balloon is pushed upward by the denser outside air. The colder—and denser—the air outside, the better your balloon will work.

As your balloon floated up, some of the hot air began to cool, and some escaped. The molecules of air inside the balloon slowed down and moved closer together. The air contracted and its volume decreased. So, the density of the air inside the balloon matched the density of the air outside. Your balloon sank because the total **weight** (WAYT) of the air inside the balloon plus the balloon materials weighed more than the air outside. Your balloon's density was greater than air.

Leonardo da Vinci and the Montgolfier brothers weren't just full of hot air when they dreamed of flying!

The French inventors, Joseph and Jacques Montgolfier, made people's dream of flight a reality in 1783 with this hot air balloon.

9

#2 HOW DID YOUR GREAT-GREAT-GREAT-GRANDMOTHER MAKE CANDY?

A long time ago, you couldn't just run to the store when you wanted candy. In some places, like on the American frontier, there was no store to run to!

Back then people had to make their own sweet treats.

What To Do

Step 1 Tie your paper clip on one end of the string. Hold the string in the glass so the paper clip rests on the bottom of the glass. Tie the other end of the string to a pencil so when the pencil rests on top of the glass, the string hangs straight and the paper clip stays on the bottom.

Step 2 Take the pencil-string-paper-clip setup out of the glass. Place some sugar on a piece of paper. Run the string under warm water. Then, rub the string in the sugar until it is coated from top to bottom. Finally, hang the setup back in the glass. (You may want to set up several glasses at once. The more setups you have, the more chances you have of getting results.)

Ask an adult to help you boil 1 cup (240 ml) of water in a small pan. When the water is boiling, keep stirring while slowly adding 2 1/2 cups (600 ml) of sugar. Be careful not to scorch, or burn, the sugar.

Step 3 When all of the sugar is dissolved, take the pan off the stove. Keep stirring a short while to make sure all of the sugar has dissolved. Then, let the sugar **solution** (suh LOO shun) cool for about 1/2 hour. After the solution has cooled, carefully pour it into your glass with the sugar-coated string. Set the glass aside where it won't be moved.

Step 4 After 2 weeks, check the glass. Has anything happened to the string? Make note of the date and any **observations** in your **science log.** You might want to sketch or take photographs of what's happening inside the glass. Check back once each week for a month.

If you find a crust forming on top of the sugar solution, carefully break through it. Transfer the string setup to another glass. Then, carefully pour the liquid solution into the new glass, keeping the solid material from getting into the new glass.

What You Need

- ✓ 2 1/2 (600 ml) cups of sugar
- ✓ water
- ✓ tall drinking glass
- ✓ cotton string
- ✓ large paper clip
- ✓ pencil
- ✓ cooking pan
- ✓ adult to help

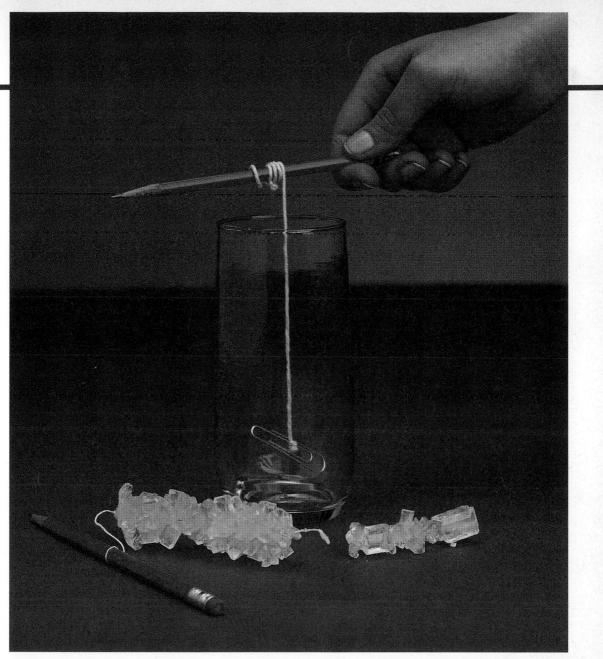

It will take several weeks to get large sugar crystals, but the wait is well worth it. Rock candy is crystallized, purified sugar—even sweeter than the sugar you buy from the store!

Is This What Happened?

Step 4: Eventually, clear **crystals** (KRIS tuhlz) should grow on your string. You made rock candy! How does it taste?

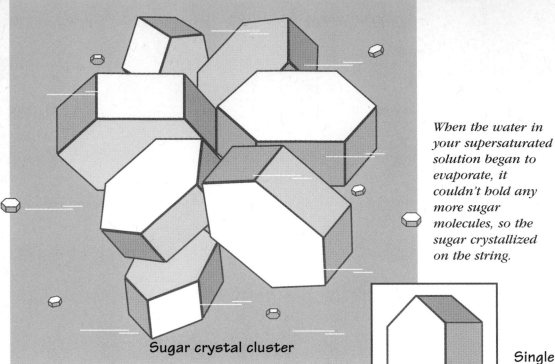

When the water in your supersaturated solution began to evaporate, it couldn't hold any more sugar molecules, so the sugar crystallized on the string.

Sugar crystal cluster

Single sugar crystal

Why?

If you tried to dissolve 2 1/2 cups (600 ml) of sugar into 1 cup (240 ml) of water right out of the faucet, what would happen? You'd have some soggy sugar. Because you boiled the water, the water **molecules** began to move faster and farther apart. Suddenly, there was more room for the sugar molecules to fit between the water molecules.

By adding the sugar to the boiling water, you created a **saturated solution** (SA chur ayt ed suh LOO shun). The water held as much sugar as it could at that temperature. When the sugar solution cooled it became a **supersaturated** (soo per SA chur ayt ed) solution, holding more sugar than water normally should at a cooler temperature.

Supersaturation is the secret to sweet rock candy. As water began to evaporate from the supersaturated solution, it couldn't hold all the sugar molecules anymore. The sugar molecules had to go somewhere, so they crystallized on your string. Over time as more water evaporated, more sugar molecules fell out of the solution and the crystals grew larger. That's why it's important to break any crust that grows on top of your glass. If you let the crust grow, evaporation can't happen and the crystals won't grow. Do you think your great-great-great-grandmother knew she was a scientist?

HOW DOES A TELEGRAPH WORK?

Can you imagine living without a telephone or computers? Until the 1840s, people living in separate towns could only communicate with hand-delivered letters. In 1837 **Samuel F.B. Morse** invented the first telegraph, and in 1844 the first telegraph message was sent from Washington, D.C., to Baltimore, Maryland.

Those first few short taps sounded the beginning of the modern age of electronic communication. Telegraphs were the fastest form of communication until the late 1800s when another invention appeared—the telephone.

What You Need

- ✓ 2 pieces of wood— 3/4 by 3 1/2 by 4 inches (1.9 by 8.9 by 10.2 cm)
- ✓ 1 piece of wood— 1/4 by 2 by 4 inches (.6 by 5 by 10.2 cm)
- ✓ galvanized iron sheet metal— 3/4 inch (1.9 cm) by 8 inches (20 cm)
- ✓ pencil
- ✓ 3 1/2-inch iron nail with flat head
- ✓ 3, 1 1/2-inch finishing nails
- ✓ 2, 1/2-inch-by-12 sheet metal screws
- ✓ 12 feet (3.7 m) bell wire— 34-gauge insulated, solid copper wire
- ✓ metal shears or heavy scissors
- ✓ sharp knife or wire stripper
- ✓ file
- ✓ 6-volt lantern battery
- ✓ adult to help

What To Do

Step 1 Get ready to build a sounder. Use three finishing nails to nail one end of the large piece of wood to the other large piece as shown in the illustration on page 15.

Step 2 Place the longest side, or base board, of the wooden "L" on the table facing you. Halfway between the side edges, measure 1 inch (2.5 cm) from the front edge of the base board and make a pencil mark. Hammer the 3 1/2-inch nail into the base board at this mark—about 1/2 inch (1.3 cm) deep.

Step 3 If your bell wire is double, separate the wires— you'll only need one. Measure 2 feet (61 cm) from one end of the wire, and leave it free. Past this 2-foot point, wrap the insulated wire tightly around the nail, starting at the bottom. Keep wrapping the wire until it reaches just below the head of the nail.

Then wrap the wire around the nail again, covering the first layer of wire, until you reach the bottom of the nail. Measure 2 feet (61 cm) of wire from the bottom of the nail, and cut the wire. Now you should have two wires coming from the bottom of the nail— the first 2 feet (61 cm) you left, and the second 2 feet (61 cm) you measured. Use a knife or wire strippers to strip about 1 inch (2.5 cm) of insulation from the ends of both wires.

Step 4 Ask an adult to help you cut a piece of sheet metal 3/4 inches (1.9 cm) by 4 inches (10.2 cm) using a metal shears or heavy scissors. Center this metal piece on the upright part of the "L." One end of this metal piece should be over the nail. Use a sheet metal screw to hold it in place. Then bend the sheet metal slightly so it is about 1/4 inch (.6 cm) away from the nail head.

Step 5 Now you'll make a key to go with your sounder. Ask an adult to help you cut a piece of sheet metal 3/4 inch (1.9 cm) by 3 1/2 inches (6.4 cm). Center this metal strip on the small piece of wood, and attach it with a sheet metal screw. Before tightening the screw all the way, place the bare end of one wire from the sounder between the screw head and the sheet metal. Then tighten.

Step 6 Carefully bend the other end of the sheet metal up so that it is 1 inch (2.5 cm) above the wood.

Cut a new piece of wire 2 feet (61 cm) long. Strip 1 inch (2.5 cm) of insulation off of each end. Underneath the bent-up metal end, use a metal screw to attach one bare end of the new wire to the small piece of wood. Check your setup against the illustration. Do all the pieces match? You should have one free wire coming from the sounder and one free wire coming from the key, which you will attach to the battery.

Step 7 Attach one free wire to the **positive** (PAH zi tiv) part of your 6-volt battery, and attach the other free wire to the **negative** (NEG ah tiv). On the key, push the bent end of the sheet metal down, so it touches the head of the sheet metal screw. What happens? Write all your **observations** in your **science log.**

Each time you tap the key, the sounder should make a clicking sound. With longer wires, you could send telegraph messages to your friend in another room, or even in another town—just like they did in the 1800s.

How to Set Up Your Telegraph

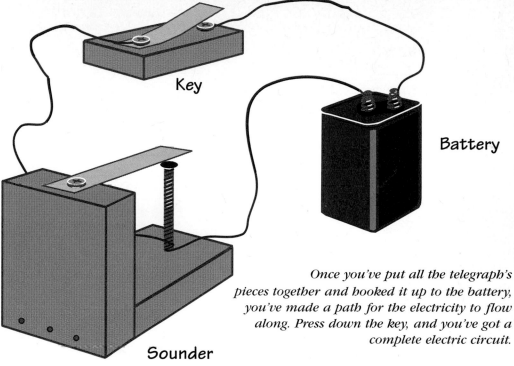

Key

Battery

Sounder

Once you've put all the telegraph's pieces together and hooked it up to the battery, you've made a path for the electricity to flow along. Press down the key, and you've got a complete electric circuit.

Is This What Happened?

Step 6: Each time you tapped the key, the sounder should have made a clicking sound.

If the sounder doesn't click, try bending the sounder's strip of metal closer to the nail head. If the sounder clicks and then sticks, try bending the sounder's strip of metal up more, farther away from the nail head.

The nail becomes a magnet only when electricity is flowing through the wires, creating a magnetic field. That makes the nail an electromagnet.

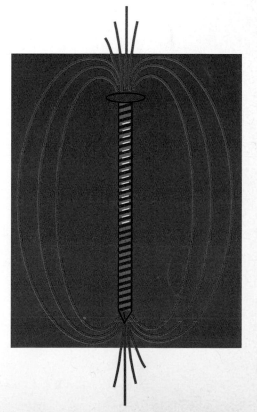

Why?

With a little help from the ideas of Samuel Morse, you've just worked out the principles of **electromagnetism** (ee lek tro MAG neh tiz um)! When you pushed the metal strip, or switch, down on your telegraph key, you completed an electric circuit. Electricity flowed from the battery through the wires to the key, through the connecting switch, to the sounder and back to the battery again.

So how does an **electric current** (ee LEK trik KER ent) make the sounder click? When electricity flows through wires, it creates a **magnetic field** (mag NET ik FEELD) around the wires. As the electricity moves through the wires wrapped around the nail, the nail becomes a magnet and attracts the sheet metal above it. Click! When you take your finger off the switch, the electric circuit is broken. The magnetic fields around the wires disappear and the nail is no longer a magnet.

To come up with his telegraph invention, Samuel Morse must have been attracted to electricity!

International Morse Code

A .-	B -...	C -.-.	D -..	E .
F ..-.	G --.	H	I ..	J .---
K -.-.	L .-..	M --	N -.	O ---
P .--.	Q --.-	R .-.	S ...	T -
U ..-	V ...-	W .--	X -..-	Y -.--
Z --..	1 .----	2 ..---	3 ...--	4 ....-
5	6 -....	7 --...	8 ---..	9 ----.
O -----				

In addition to inventing the telegraph, Samuel Morse invented a system to spell words using tapping sounds. A dash — is a tap and a short pause before the next tap. A dot • is a tap and no pause. You can use Morse Code to send messages with the telegraph you build.

HOW CAN YOU USE THE SUN TO TELL TIME?

People didn't start using clocks, as we know them, until the 14th and 15th centuries. Before clocks and watches existed, people used the sun and the shadows it cast to tell time.

A sundial used by the ancient Egyptians still works today. Even George Washington carried a pocket sundial!

What To Do

Step 1 You need to find out the **latitude** (LAT i tood) of where you live and where *true north* is. (True north is not the same as magnetic north. Your compass will show you magnetic north. True north may lie in a slightly different direction than magnetic north, depending on where you live.) Try calling your city or county engineer or surveyor, or call the public library. You could also ask an adult to help you find this information on a topographic map of your area.

Step 2 Ask an adult to help you cut two pieces of cardboard from a box— 6 inches (15.2 cm) by 9 inches (22.9 cm). Spray one side of each piece with flat white spray paint and let it dry. Before you paint, be sure to read and follow all the caution notes and directions on the paint can.

Spray a second coat of paint over the first. After the pieces dry, flip them over and paint two coats on the other side, too.

What You Need

- ✓ 2 pieces of corrugated cardboard—6 inches (15.2 cm) by 9 inches (22.9 cm)
- ✓ flat white spray paint
- ✓ 1/8-inch (.3-cm) wood dowel, or rod—11 inches (27.9 cm) long
- ✓ drawing compass
- ✓ magnetic compass
- ✓ straight pin or sewing pin
- ✓ protractor
- ✓ ruler
- ✓ black ball-point pen for compass
- ✓ black fine-point permanent marker
- ✓ hobby knife
- ✓ masking tape
- ✓ clock or watch set to local time
- ✓ adult to help

Step 3 Place the cardboard so the 6-inch (15.2-cm) sides are at the top and bottom. Using your ruler, find the point on your cardboard 4 inches (10.2 cm) from the bottom and 3 inches (7.6 cm) from either side. Make a pencil mark.

Set your drawing compass to draw a 5-inch (12.7-cm) circle and put on a black ball-point pen. Place the point of your compass on your pencil mark and draw a circle.

Step 4 With your fine-point pen, draw a line 4 inches (10.2 cm) from the bottom of the cardboard, from one side of your circle to the other. This line should go through the mark you made in Step 3.

Place your protractor on this line, curved side down. Make a pencil mark every 15 degrees. You should end up with 11 marks—at 15°, 30°, 45°, 60°, 75°, 90°, 75°, 60°, 45°, 30°, 15°. Draw lines from the center point of your circle, through each mark to the outside of the circle. These lines represent the daylight hours. Label the line coming straight down from the circle's center "12." To the left of this line, working your way up to the side, label the lines starting with "1" through "6." These lines show the p.m. hours. To the right, start with "11" and go backwards to "6." These are the a.m. hours. Write "Spring and Summer" at the top of the cardboard. This is your upper dial plate.

Use a protractor to make a mark every 15 degrees. Then draw a line from the center of the circle, through each mark. Each line represents one hour in a day.

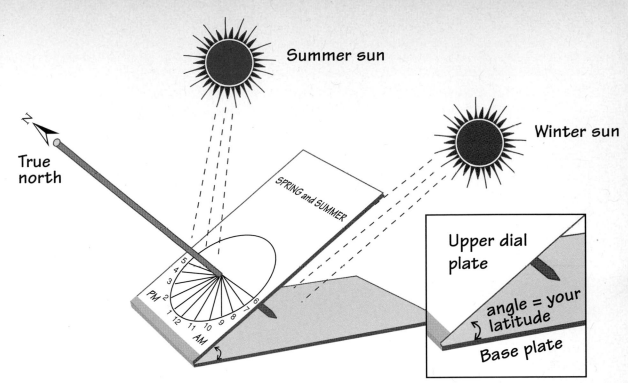

Because the sun's position in the sky changes with the seasons, the summer and spring sun shines on the upper dial plate, and the winter and fall sun shines on the lower dial plate. To make your sundial as accurate as you can, make sure the angle between the dial plate and base plate is equal to your latitude.

Step 5 Use the point of a straight pin to make a hole through the cardboard at the circle's center point. On the opposite side of the cardboard, repeat Step 3 and Step 4 using the pin hole as the center point for your new circle. On this circle the p.m. hours will be to the right and the a.m. hours will be to your left. On this side, write "Fall and Winter" at the top of the cardboard. This is your lower dial plate.

Tape the bottom edge of the dial plate to the other piece of cardboard, using masking tape. Make sure that the "Spring and Summer" side is up. The bottom piece is called the base plate.

Step 6 Ask an adult to help you sharpen one end of the wood rod, or dowel—just like a pencil. Hold the dial plate away from the base plate. Carefully push the pointed end of the rod through the center of the circle so it comes through the center of the circle on the other side. This part of a sundial is called a *gnomon*.

Did you remember to write down the latitude of where you live? Find the angle of your latitude on your protractor. Push the dial plate up or down the gnomon until the angle between the dial plate and the base plate matches your latitude. Then set the point of the gnomon on the base plate and push so it stays in place. Check the angle between the gnomon at the top of the dial plate—it should be 90°.

Step 7 Take your sundial out on a sunny day. Set it on a level surface. Use your magnetic compass to find north. Then use the information you gathered in Step 1 to find true north, and point the gnomon in that direction.

If it is spring or summer, look on the upper dial. If it is autumn or winter, look on the lower dial. Write down your **observations** in your **science log.** You may want to photograph or videotape your sundial for several seconds, every hour throughout the day.

Is This What Happened?

Step 7: You should see the shadow of the gnomon on the hour line (or near it), just like the hour hand on a clock or watch. But if it's daylight savings time, the sundial will be an hour off.

If it is spring or summer, the shadow should be on the upper dial. If it is fall or winter, the shadow should be on the lower dial.

If you have trouble setting your sundial to tell the right time, try going out when you know it is 12 noon. Set your sundial so the gnomon's shadow falls over the 12 mark. Then watch to see how well your sundial keeps time!

Why?

Your sundial is really a mini-model of the Earth! The equator goes around the Earth in an imaginary circle—a circle like you drew for your dial plate. There are 360 degrees in a circle and 24 hours in a day. If you divide 360 by 24, you get 15. Sound familiar? The hour lines on your sundial are 15 degrees apart.

When you set your sundial at the same angle as the latitude where you live and pointed it toward true north, as far as the sun was concerned, there was no difference between the equator and your dial. As the Earth **rotates** (ROH tayts) on its **axis** (AKS iss), the sun appears to move—about 15 degrees per hour.

In summer the northern hemisphere of the Earth is tilted toward the sun, so the sun appears north of your latitude. The light of the sun will fall on the upper dial plate. In winter it is tilted away, so the sun appears farther south, and the light will fall on the lower dial plate.

If you can get the right angle on it, telling time by the sun is a breeze.

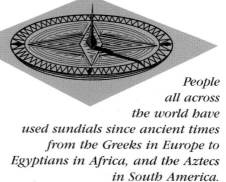

People all across the world have used sundials since ancient times from the Greeks in Europe to Egyptians in Africa, and the Aztecs in South America.

5

ROURKE
SCIENCE
PROJECTS

HOW DID OUR ANCESTORS DYE CLOTH?

A long time ago, brightly colored clothing was not common. And fluorescent? Forget it. Only the very rich could afford the rich reds, yellows and purples that we see in stores every day.

Most clothing colors we look for today come from chemical dyes discovered in laboratories. Our ancestors had to make do with colors they found in nature.

What To Do

Step 1 Cut four 6-inch (15.2-cm) squares of wool. Use a permanent marking pen to mark the corner of one square "AB" for alum-blueberry. Mark another "AT" for alum-tea, "B" for blueberry and "T" for tea.

Put all of the pieces of wool in a pot and add 1 quart (1 liter) of water. Ask an adult to help you bring the water to a boil. As soon as the water boils, take the pot from the heat and let the wool cool for 1 hour. Then hang the wool to let it dry.

Step 2 In a pot add 2 heaping teaspoons (10 ml) of **alum** (AL um) to 1 quart (1 liter) of water. Bring the water to a boil and add the wool marked "AB" and "AT." Reduce the heat and let the wool simmer, or boil gently, in the alum and water for 1 hour. Then let it cool. Finally, hang the pieces up to drip dry. Do not wring them.

Step 3 In a pot add 10 teaspoons (50 ml) of tea to 1 1/2 quarts (1.5 liters) of water, and bring it to a boil. You will have to stir the mixture so it doesn't boil over. Then reduce the heat and simmer the tea for 10 minutes.

What You Need

✓ white or off-white wool cloth (available at fabric stores)
✓ scissors
✓ water
✓ loose tea leaves
✓ fresh or frozen blueberries
✓ blender or potato masher
✓ several bowls
✓ alum (available at grocery stores)
✓ 2-quart (2-liter), or larger, cooking pots
✓ black, permanent marking pen
✓ string
✓ soap or detergent
✓ strainer
✓ adult to help

Many different kinds of plants and berries can be, and were, used to dye clothing. Our ancestors had to spin sheep's wool into yarn, which they dyed and made into clothes for their families.

Step 4 With the help of an adult, carefully strain the tea into a bowl. Throw the tea leaves away and rinse the pot. Then, pour the strained tea back into the pot and bring it to a boil. Put in the wool marked "T" and reduce the heat. Cover the pot and simmer for 15 minutes.

Use a fork or spoon to take the wool out of the hot tea. Place the wool in a bowl and run warm water over it. Rinse the wool until no color comes out with the water. Then wring it out and hang it to dry. Repeat Step 3 and Step 4 using the wool marked "AT." What happens to the wool? Write all your **observations** in your **science log.**

Step 5 Using a blender or potato masher, crush 1 to 1 1/2 cups (240 to 360 ml), or 8 to 12 ounces (227 to 340 grams) of blueberries. In a pot add the blueberry mush to 1 1/2 quarts (1.5 to 2 liters) of water. Then follow Steps 3 and 4 using the blueberry mush instead of the tea. First treat the wool marked "B," then "AB." What does the wool look like? Are there any differences? Describe what you see in your science log.

Step 6 Hand wash each piece of wool separately in very warm water with soap or detergent. Rinse each in hot water until no suds come out with the water. Then, hang the pieces to dry.

Wash and dry the pieces several times. What happens? Write down your observations. You may want to take photographs for your final display.

Step 7 Try crushing other berries or plants to use as dyes. Some jellies and jams may work as well. Follow all the steps with some pieces, and with others, skip Step 2. What happens? Try using cotton pieces instead of wool pieces. What's the difference?

Is This What Happened?

Steps 4-5: Both pieces of wool dyed in tea should have been a reddish brown color. The wool dyed in blueberries should have been grayish purple. "B" might have been a little lighter in color than "AB."

Step 6: After one washing, both pieces of tea-dyed wool should have looked pretty much the same as before. On the other hand, the blueberry-dyed "B" should have gotten much lighter than "AB."

Step 7: Some colored berries work better than others to dye your cloth. If you tried cotton, you should have noticed that cotton does not hold color as well as wool.

After rinsing the wool, wring it out and hang it up to dry. Which worked as the better dye—tea or blueberries?

Many berries and plants work as dyes. This chart shows the colors produced by common plants. Would you guess that dandelions would dye cloth magenta?

The labels on the chart read: onions, sunflowers, goldenrod, birch leaves, cornflowers, dandelions

Why?

When people first started to dye cloth, the colors faded quickly. But they found out that if they boiled it, or treated the cloth another way, it would hold color longer. Later they discovered that if you treat cloth with alum or other substances, the color would stay even longer.

Substances that help dyes stay in cloth are called **mordants** (MOR dents). Mordants help to chemically bind dyes to cloth. They work sort of like glue.

Some ancient peoples and the early Native Americans found that treating wool with clay before dying it helped the cloth stay colorful longer. Clay contains aluminum compounds—like the alum you used in Step 2. Alum acts as a mordant for wool. Without it the blueberry color washes out.

Why didn't the tea-dyed wool not treated with alum fade? A compound in tea called *tannin* works as a mordant as well as a dye. By boiling wool in tea, you were dying it and treating it with a mordant at the same time, so both pieces stayed brown—even after washing.

6

HOW CAN YOU MAKE LIGHTNING JUMP FROM A BALLOON?

In 1747, **Benjamin Franklin** got the idea that lightning was a form of electricity. But it wasn't until 1752 that he got around to testing this **hypothesis** by flying a kite during a thunderstorm.

His experiment was a very dangerous one. Two other people who tried it were electrocuted! There are many safer ways to experiment with electricity.

What To Do

Step 1 Find a room that you can keep pretty dark. Blow up a balloon almost as big as it will get and tie it off. Be careful not to overfill the balloon. If it pops, small pieces of the balloon could get into your eyes.

Step 2 Ask a friend to make **observations** during your experiment, or go through the steps in front of a mirror. Darken the room. Then rub the balloon as hard and fast as you can against a wool cloth or your hair. What do you hear? What do you see? Repeat this several times. Ask your friend to rub the balloon. Write your observations down in your **science log.**

Step 3 With the help of an adult, set the fluorescent tube on a flat surface. Tape the tube down around its middle so it stays in place. Darken the room and rub a blown-up balloon against cloth. Then, slowly and carefully bring the balloon very close to—but do not touch—one end of the fluorescent tube. What do you hear and see? Try this several times. Write down your observations.

What You Need

✓ round balloons
✓ 15-watt, 18-inch (45.7-cm) fluorescent tube, or light
✓ wool, or fuzzy, cloth
✓ tape
✓ friend to help
✓ adult to help

What does crazy-looking hair have to do with lightning? When you rub a balloon on your head you're building up an electrical charge on the balloon, just like falling raindrops build up a charge in thunderclouds.

Is This What Happened?

Step 2: You should have heard a crackling noise. If the room was dark enough, you might have even seen sparks.

Step 3: You should have heard a loud snap, or a crackling sound. At the same time, the fluorescent tube should have flashed!

Why?

When you rubbed the balloon with the cloth, some of the **atoms** (A tuhmz) in the balloon material picked up **electrons** (ee LEK tronz) from the atoms of the cloth material. Electrons are tiny, **negatively-charged** particles that go around the nucleus, or center, of an atom. When they moved onto the balloon material, it became negatively charged.

The same sort of thing happens in thunderclouds. The raindrops rub against the moving air in the cloud, and the cloud picks up electrons—becoming negatively charged. The ground becomes **positively** charged. Opposite charges attract, and when the charges in the clouds and the ground get strong enough— zap!—electrons jump from the negative clouds to the positive ground in a flash of lightning.

That's just what you saw—on a smaller scale—when the spark jumped from your balloon to the fluorescent tube. Since you know that it's electricity that makes fluorescent tubes glow, with this experiment you've proven that lightning, large or small, is really a form of electricity. Ben Franklin would have been proud of you—positively!

When the negative charges in the clouds and the positive charges in the ground get strong enough—zap!—electrons jump from the clouds to the ground in a flash of lightning.

HOW TO DISPLAY YOUR PROJECT

When you finish your project, your teacher may ask you to share it with your class or show it at a science fair. Professional scientists often show their work to other people. Here are some tips on how to display your project.

Many students show their projects with a three-board, free-standing display. Before you start putting everything together, make a sketch of how you would like your display to look. This is the best time to make changes.

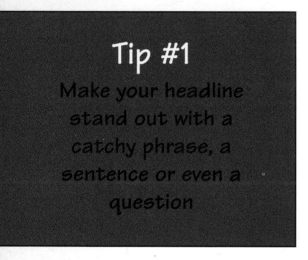

Tip #1

Make your headline stand out with a catchy phrase, a sentence or even a question

The title of your project should attract people's attention. It could be one or two words—a catchy phrase, a sentence or even a question. Use the largest lettering for your title. In your display, you should also state the scientific problem you were trying to solve. Use a question, like the chapter titles in this book, or state your problem in the form of a **hypothesis.**

If you have a computer of your own, or can use one at school, they work great for lettering. Or, you can neatly print on a white sheet of paper, and border your lettering with colored construction paper to make it stand out.

You'll also need to leave room to display the most important part of your project—your results. Show any photographs, drawings, charts, graphs or tables—anything that will help to explain what you've learned. You can use

Tip #2

Use color on graphs and charts

black marker to make tables and charts, and colored marker for graphs. If you're handy with a computer, you might try to make your graphs and charts with a computer program!

Tip #3
Label everything clearly

Once you have all the pieces, tape everything into place. Follow the sketch you drew. Using tape will let you rearrange things until your display looks exactly how you want it. Then glue the pieces permanently.

As part of your exhibit, you'll want to include your **science log** and final report, along with any equipment you used, or models you made. Make sure your report is easy to read—neatly printed or typed. Be sure to label everything clearly.

Finally, you'll want to be able to tell people about your project. Practice what you want to say beforehand as many times as you can. Tell your parents, a friend, or even your dog about it. Then when a teacher or judge asks you about your project, you'll know what to say. You can share what you've discovered, and show that science really is part of everyone's life. After all, you've just become a real scientist!

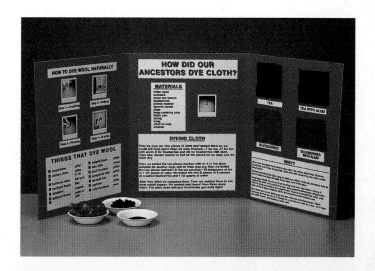

Sharing your results is an important part of being a scientist. A well-organized display will make explaining what you've learned easier.

GLOSSARY

alchemist (AL kem ist) – early scientists who tried to change lead into gold and make people's lives longer; 16th- and 17th-century chemists

alum (AL um) – saltlike chemicals made up of aluminum, sulfur and oxygen

atom (A tuhm) – the smallest part of an element that has the properties of, or acts and reacts like, that element; made up of electrons and a nucleus—protons and neutrons

axis (AKS iss) – an imaginary line passing through the Earth from the north pole to the south pole; the Earth rotates around its axis

Benjamin Franklin (1706-1790) – American scientist and inventor, statesman, printer, author

crystal (KRIS tuhl) – a solid found in nature that has a specific shape with a repeating pattern of sides and angles

density (DEN sih tee) – weight per unit volume; a pound of feathers and a pound of lead both weigh the same, but the pound of feathers takes up more space—it has less density than lead

electric current (ee LEK trik KER ent) – flow of electrons along a conductor

electromagnetism (ee lek tro MAG neh tiz um) – process of producing a magnetic field by using an electric current; an electromagnet is only a magnet when electricity is flowing

electrons (ee LEK tronz) – negatively-charged particles that go around the outside of the positively-charged center of atoms

hypothesis (hii POTH uh siss) – a possible answer to a scientific question; sometimes called an educated guess because scientists use what they *already* know to guess how the experiment will turn out

latitude (LAT i tood) – distance in degrees north or south of the equator

Leonardo da Vinci (1452-1519) – Italian artist, scientist, engineer, inventor

magnetic field (mag NET ik FEELD) – space around a magnet, or something carrying an electric current that is magnetic

molecule (MAHL i kyool) – the smallest part of a substance (element or compound) that has the properties of that substance; H_2 represents a molecule of hydrogen (an element), and H_2O represents a molecule of water (a compound)

Montgolfier brothers (Joseph 1740-1810, Jacques 1745-1799) – French inventors

mordant (MOR dent) – any substance used to pre-treat fabric for dyeing; any substance used to bind a dye to a fabric

negative (NEG ah tiv) – having extra electrons, or more electrons than protons—positively-charged particles in atoms

observation (ahb zer VAY shun) – information gathered by carefully using your senses; seeing, hearing, touching, smelling and tasting

positive (PAH zi tiv) – having fewer electrons than protons—positively-charged particles in atoms

rotate (ROH tayt) – to turn around a center point; the Earth rotates on its axis

Samuel F.B. Morse (1791-1872) – American inventor and artist

saturated solution (SA chur ayt ed suh LOO shun) – a solution in which the solvent (the dissolver) holds as much of the solute (the dissolvee) as it can at a certain temperature

science log (SII ens LAWG) – a notebook that includes the title of your project, the date you started, your list of materials, procedures you followed with dates and times, your observations and results

Sir Isaac Newton (1642-1727) - English scientist and mathematician

solution (suh LOO shun) – a mixture in which all parts are mixed evenly throughout; a solution will not settle out and cannot be separated by filtering

supersaturated (soo per SA chur ayt ed) – holding more solute—substance being dissolved—than normal at a given temperature

volume (VAHL yoom) – the amount of space an object takes up; how big, in all directions, something is

weight (WAYT) – the measure of the force of gravity acting on an object

INDEX